# Glint

Carole Symer

Dear Anne-Marie,

Thanks to you & Katey & Holey, the glint in my eyes is Restored. May you always have yours handy.

With so much gratitude

Carole

Harbor Editions
Small Harbor Publishing

Cover art by Billy Renkl
Cover design by Katie Tandy
Book layout by Cameron Morse, Hannah Martin, Allison Blevins

GLINT
CAROLE SYMER
ISBN 978-1-7359090-4-2
Harbor Editions,
an imprint of Small Harbor Publishing

*] heart*
*]absolutely*
*]I can*
*]*
*]would be for me*
*]to shine in answer*
*]face*
*]*
*]having been stained*
*]*

—Sappho, Fragment 4

# CONTENTS

# Glint

# i.

wouldn't it be just like our baby
to come on a Sunday in August traffic
you mimicking Nurse Ratched
and me relieved it wasn't my sister's cooking
that poisoned the evening

swooning under yellow hospital light
for one more lick of ice

and you Tesoro

oddly content with cold hospital ziti

## ii.

so much of the world inside

sipped through the nipple
ready to read saliva
ready to read a mother's antibodies

I tell our baby Don't let anyone
suck the language of water out of you
or erase the backwash inside

the world's waters
your mother's sacred
huge outrageous rivers wrap you

# iii.

before the rice turns translucent
before vanilla flecks fragrant with milk
and sugar

before silky oozie
                              us [again
ready to devour
                              over low flame]

melted back into kids

## iv.

did you smell like Earl Grey and honey
when you were our girl's sweet age of five
or whiffs of fresh cut grass and olive oil?

with time the scent of human-soft
reconfigures     again
                              again

as we travel down ageless protoplasmic
thin blue lines of electric space

how do any of us smell human at all?

## V.

I hate my breasts how round my shoulders
like a mystical moon's trickeries

a hive of voices
enter cold dark matter

another baby, your baby coming along
as she does

[from your mouth to] where stars are
your idiom already inside

## vi.

these     our bodies
      like primordial jellyfish
dreaming with volume up

# vii.

how after rain smells—
when flesh feels most savage
you glean
                my sweat      my steam
claim I'm too intense   too awake
to make a home out of a rising body count

far outside my skin   tepid
you run from my emotional velocity
a graining of sense I swear

## viii.

your body now smoke—
heat gone in a
glance of arctic air

# ix.

take 91 straight up through Deerfield
and as we pass Putney
you imagine the lift under your skis

I have a moment too
seeing light return to your face
the smell of fresh pine
try to picture a horizon that bends

nothing ever a straight line

# X.

you see me lift my breast a little to the left
so this man can get by me on a crowded train

the pulsating rhythms
the daily clank
of bowls and plates
fluent in things vulnerable like

subways        lightning        whitewater

a rare melt of your face
like a January sun
I too can hide

fetching [don't you think?]
chicken from deep freeze
thighs and breasts on a bed of white rice

after all I've been through
you got me        [lying
a new idiom, is it not?]
legs spread on white sheets

# xi.

I do not want to be weaned by age
or Stepford wives dreaming themselves
erotic. There's only so much
snow one can suppress.

Bring me the last of the rosé
all you luminous souls
and I will speak of marriage and of
the two maybe three times
I felt most deliciously female.

# xii.

why when winter
deer no longer paw soft pine

generations of beetles and geese
wandered valiantly
beneath a frozen sky

reminds us we too can adapt
inside a heartbeat

earth-body stay warm

this is the brilliance
a sanguine blood moon

that each fawn
each fir each one of us
takes to find each other

and yes we said these things all night long
if ever before we did love

but we were young and famished
not knowing how to see a field of dying grass

# xiii.

when the light is low
when darkness feels like a fresh start

for restraint to thin out loud
a couple of vowels

odd and personal
to say why not

❋

there in that gaze
          the glint you didn't get

you gave our girls
what Darwin and Machin
found holy
                    moly
in a tumble
               and tickle

to heighten the play
               in gamma waves
the whiff of a baby
     birth of oxytocin
                    even an ape-
daddy can learn
          to love        is to survive

# xiv.

when sleet is all the sky would spare
when lines of peeling birch

gray     serious pine

far back beyond rock
when once     our trees
    coyote wail
a dried-up riverbed

where so little persists
where once you     but not fallow

while the world in me no longer warm
your snore insists on being
what else pleases throat and ear

❀

and

      and

after the heat dies     does it hover
for a while like cloud shreds
or kiss the treetops
before final ascent

❀

too bad about our marriage by the way
I never thanked you
for your lesson on scud-runners and
the value of an accurate flight manifest
I should have listened

## XV.

how you would have loved
me in one slow BDSM
unravel after

                              a second alarm rings
while I stumble downstairs to brew coffee
the scent of burnt burns me and
I wrap my fingers around
the neck of your *Go, Blue* mug

to make my way back
to dream of other ways

to love how you will

# xvi.

on the night in February that shall remain
unnumbered and nameless

miso soup suggests Nigel Slater will do
the trick with a small scoop of yellow paste
added to boiling water. You must
throw in anything you care to discard
by which he means mushrooms
noodles and Chinese greens

but tonight I toss in
two once-ecstatic hearts
now etherized
the tail of a smarmy bastard
a couple of straying souls
a long-chain of kisses and roads
taken then abandoned
luring you forward

knowing there are times when you want
something spicy and hot
and appetite gets the better of conscience

until a twist of the old knife
and a poke with a fork—

## xvii.

let lingering let rage let tongue

and yes to touch
your skin pushed into
                              no
                                        wait
grab a pencil with an eraser

more like every part of you
marooned with mine

in another room
                    under the stairwell
back of a Buick Skylark

let all this entrance and love too
                              ruin us

# xviii.

wherever you
go garrulous go young

yellow warbler
sweeten the dark

tell me the effort it takes
to feel your way through

to return again      to spring
to inhale greening earth

everywhere you

# xix.

I in red gingham am
my gramma's child
so proud
so loved

still a kid [I kid you not] my first husband
was a little rigid
let's just say like Hannah Gadsby
but seriously not
as whip-smart nor funny

the smell of fresh rosemary
and orange peel
the push I need
to harness the heat within

## XX.

remember wanting? acid and moisture
that summer when the air was thick
and in cahoots
                    like a hard yellow heat
then rain             rips me to shreds
beautiful
                  you
beside the twisted pine
waiting to carry your fury over rock and snake

and I a shape with so much space around me

O to only    O to awaken    O to another way
to fix oats

trees too need space—their shy crowns
refuse to touch
                      night after night
the cellular tissue between tree bark and
wood swells
                        until dawn
and the pores of leaves open

## xxi.

yes, you—that's right
you Tesoro
my second      okay technically
my third love

you gave us much to worry
but you are gold
our golden boy
you played the part
like only Pacino could

after summer passed on

the scent of hyacinth
comes wafting back
as you do now

# xxii.

if you close your eyes Tesoro
imagine

a thin green line
follows a field

navy then white like cotton

bird cries drown the quiet
it almost hurts to hear

how we moved on
from so much flesh

beneath the cosmic gauze
pulsing pulsing purple

minutes before
a pink dawn

like skin
turned way down

from summer's heat

hydrangea   nettle   beach plums

let it be enough

## xxiii.

if this dress
this heart
were a field
of clover
soaked in sun

and you
a summer visitor
nose to bloom

I'd still have
to call on
purple impatiens

until we in-
hale and be healed

# xxiv.

I am a woman
snapped open
feverish to all that is
unleaving us

this time a warbler
misreads glass
as the splendor of oak
ablaze with autumn

wings splayed
air parting for the awful
glint of heaven

I wait over her body
to be sure the cat doesn't
haul her off first

this time to say
what if I'm not
too late to rescue

## XXV.

love, spill open
one piece at a time
a wish threaded through
a heart a breast a womb if you will

shamanic release phantastical

the longing to be a birch
alongside soft pine maybe a spruce or two

down the field where the grass is bent

the dark secret love we bear
like a fallen log in the forest

of all the altars on display
I am happiest to be a standing wave
wrapped with you [yes,     you]
in a rainbow mala

# ACKNOWLEDGMENTS

Many thanks to the editors who first published my poems. You urged me to keep writing "what love looks like many years in," which inspired this collection to take shape.

> *Mutha Magazine*: an earlier version of "ii" as "so much of the world inside"

> *Wild Roof Journal*: an earlier version of "xxii" as "when the beach plums are scarlet"

Sappho, translated by Anne Carson, is quoted from *If Not, Winter: Fragments of Sappho*, New York: Vintage Books, 2002.

Cameron Morse and Allison Blevins at Small Harbor Publishing: You saw what I made and encouraged it further. Thank you for your editorial guidance and for treating me so kindly.

Thank you, Billy Renkl, for the beautiful collage on the cover.

Gratitude to Holly Wren Spaulding for planting many seeds that became poems.

Heartfelt thanks to Katey Schultz and Anne-Marie Oomen for a scholarship to Interlochen College of Creative Arts, offering me a place at the table among other writers to finish a few of these poems.

Amber Edmondson, Brit Washburn, Sharon Oriel, Moira Walsh, Janie James, and our Mr. Barrett: Thank you for your words, friendship and gracious attention to this poet and her poems.

My deepest gratitude goes to David, Christine, and Liya, whose poetry has remained my stay, my soft pine.

# ABOUT THE AUTHOR

Carole Symer is a practicing psychologist in Ann Arbor, Michigan, where she works with adolescents and young adults, from whom she learns the exquisite effort it takes to language a life. Symer also teaches at New York University and has authored nearly a thousand neuropsychological evaluations to help neurodiverse learners fulfill their civil and human rights and discover more pleasure in daily life.

Symer's essays, articles, and poems have appeared in *Across the Margin*, *Mutha Magazine*, *Black Fox Literary Magazine*, *Wild Roof Journal*, *Sky Island Journal*, *The Passed Note*, *Michigan Chronicle*, and elsewhere. She is the 2020 recipient of the Anne-Marie Oomen & Katey Schultz ICCA Creative Writing Scholarship.

Made in the USA
Monee, IL
18 July 2021

73847298R00025